# Copyright 2021

## Berkshire Hall & Epping Press

All rights reserved.

No part of this book may be produced in any written,
electronic, recording or photocopying form without the
permission of the author.

Today
is a
new
day

You
got
this!

This book belongs to: _______________

# Monthly Planner

Goals

Month:

Notes

| Mon | Tue | Wed | Thu | Fri | Sat | Sun |
|-----|-----|-----|-----|-----|-----|-----|
|  |  |  |  |  |  |  |
|  |  |  |  |  |  |  |
|  |  |  |  |  |  |  |
|  |  |  |  |  |  |  |
|  |  |  |  |  |  |  |

# Book Lists To Read

| ✓ | BOOK TITLE | AUTHOR | PROGRESS |
|---|---|---|---|
| | | | |
| | | | |
| | | | |
| | | | |
| | | | |
| | | | |
| | | | |
| | | | |
| | | | |
| | | | |

## TODAY'S SCHEDULE

| Time | |
|------|---|
| 6-7 AM | |
| 7-8 AM | |
| 8-9 AM | |
| 9-10 AM | |
| 10-11 AM | |
| 11-12 AM | |
| 12-1 PM | |
| 1-2 PM | |
| 2-3 PM | |
| 3-4 PM | |
| 4-5 PM | |
| 6-7 PM | |
| 7-8 PM | |
| 8-9 PM | |

## TOP PRIORITIES

## TO DO LIST..

☐
☐
☐
☐
☐
☐
☐
☐

## FOR TOMORROW..

## NOTE..

DATE

QUOTE FOR THE DAY

## TODAY'S SCHEDULE

6-7 AM

7-8 AM

8-9 AM

9-10 AM

10-11 AM

11-12 AM

12-1 PM

1-2 PM

2-3 PM

3-4 PM

4-5 PM

6-7 PM

7-8 PM

8-9 PM

## TOP PRIORITIES

### TO DO LIST..

## FOR TOMORROW..

## NOTE..

DATE

QUOTE FOR THE DAY

## TODAY'S SCHEDULE

| | |
|---|---|
| 6-7 AM | |
| 7-8 AM | |
| 8-9 AM | |
| 9-10 AM | |
| 10-11 AM | |
| 11-12 AM | |
| 12-1 PM | |
| 1-2 PM | |
| 2-3 PM | |
| 3-4 PM | |
| 4-5 PM | |
| 6-7 PM | |
| 7-8 PM | |
| 8-9 PM | |

## TOP PRIORITIES

FOR TOMORROW..

NOTE..

DATE

QUOTE FOR THE DAY

## ODAY'S SCHEDULE

| | |
|---|---|
| 6-7 AM | |
| 7-8 AM | |
| 8-9 AM | |
| 9-10 AM | |
| 10-11 AM | |
| 11-12 AM | |
| 12-1 PM | |
| 1-2 PM | |
| 2-3 PM | |
| 3-4 PM | |
| 4-5 PM | |
| 6-7 PM | |
| 7-8 PM | |
| 8-9 PM | |

## TOP PRIORITIES

### TO DO LIST..

## FOR TOMORROW..

## NOTE..

DATE

QUOTE FOR THE DAY

## TODAY'S SCHEDULE

| 6-7 AM | |
| 7-8 AM | |
| 8-9 AM | |
| 9-10 AM | |
| 10-11 AM | |
| 11-12 AM | |
| 12-1 PM | |
| 1-2 PM | |
| 2-3 PM | |
| 3-4 PM | |
| 4-5 PM | |
| 6-7 PM | |
| 7-8 PM | |
| 8-9 PM | |

## TOP PRIORITIES

## TO DO LIST..

## FOR TOMORROW..

## NOTE..

DATE

QUOTE FOR THE DAY

## ODAY'S SCHEDULE

| | |
|---|---|
| 6-7 AM | |
| 7-8 AM | |
| 8-9 AM | |
| 9-10 AM | |
| 10-11 AM | |
| 11-12 AM | |
| 12-1 PM | |
| 1-2 PM | |
| 2-3 PM | |
| 3-4 PM | |
| 4-5 PM | |
| 6-7 PM | |
| 7-8 PM | |
| 8-9 PM | |

## TOP PRIORITIES

### TO DO LIST..

☐
☐
☐
☐
☐
☐
☐
☐

## FOR TOMORROW..

## NOTE..

## TODAY'S SCHEDULE

| | |
|---|---|
| 6-7 AM | |
| 7-8 AM | |
| 8-9 AM | |
| 9-10 AM | |
| 10-11 AM | |
| 11-12 AM | |
| 12-1 PM | |
| 1-2 PM | |
| 2-3 PM | |
| 3-4 PM | |
| 4-5 PM | |
| 6-7 PM | |
| 7-8 PM | |
| 8-9 PM | |

## TOP PRIORITIES

## TO DO LIST..

## FOR TOMORROW..

## NOTE..

DATE

QUOTE FOR THE DAY

## TODAY'S SCHEDULE

| | |
|---|---|
| 6-7 AM | |
| 7-8 AM | |
| 8-9 AM | |
| 9-10 AM | |
| 10-11 AM | |
| 11-12 AM | |
| 12-1 PM | |
| 1-2 PM | |
| 2-3 PM | |
| 3-4 PM | |
| 4-5 PM | |
| 6-7 PM | |
| 7-8 PM | |
| 8-9 PM | |

## TOP PRIORITIES

## TO DO LIST..

## FOR TOMORROW..

## NOTE..

DATE

QUOTE FOR THE DAY

## TODAY'S SCHEDULE

| | |
|---|---|
| 6-7 AM | |
| 7-8 AM | |
| 8-9 AM | |
| 9-10 AM | |
| 10-11 AM | |
| 11-12 AM | |
| 12-1 PM | |
| 1-2 PM | |
| 2-3 PM | |
| 3-4 PM | |
| 4-5 PM | |
| 6-7 PM | |
| 7-8 PM | |
| 8-9 PM | |

## TOP PRIORITIES

## FOR TOMORROW..

NOTE..

DATE

QUOTE FOR THE DAY

## ODAY'S SCHEDULE

| | |
|---|---|
| 6-7 AM | |
| 7-8 AM | |
| 8-9 AM | |
| 9-10 AM | |
| 10-11 AM | |
| 11-12 AM | |
| 12-1 PM | |
| 1-2 PM | |
| 2-3 PM | |
| 3-4 PM | |
| 4-5 PM | |
| 6-7 PM | |
| 7-8 PM | |
| 8-9 PM | |

## TOP PRIORITIES

## TO DO LIST..

## FOR TOMORROW..

## NOTE..

DATE

QUOTE FOR THE DAY

## TODAY'S SCHEDULE

| | |
|---|---|
| 6-7 AM | |
| 7-8 AM | |
| 8-9 AM | |
| 9-10 AM | |
| 10-11 AM | |
| 11-12 AM | |
| 12-1 PM | |
| 1-2 PM | |
| 2-3 PM | |
| 3-4 PM | |
| 4-5 PM | |
| 6-7 PM | |
| 7-8 PM | |
| 8-9 PM | |

## TOP PRIORITIES

TO DO LIST..

FOR TOMORROW..

NOTE..

DATE

QUOTE FOR THE DAY

## TODAY'S SCHEDULE

| | |
|---|---|
| 6-7 AM | |
| 7-8 AM | |
| 8-9 AM | |
| 9-10 AM | |
| 10-11 AM | |
| 11-12 AM | |
| 12-1 PM | |
| 1-2 PM | |
| 2-3 PM | |
| 3-4 PM | |
| 4-5 PM | |
| 6-7 PM | |
| 7-8 PM | |
| 8-9 PM | |

## TOP PRIORITIES

## TO DO LIST..

## FOR TOMORROW..

## NOTE..

DATE

QUOTE FOR THE DAY

## TODAY'S SCHEDULE

| 6-7 AM | |
| 7-8 AM | |
| 8-9 AM | |
| 9-10 AM | |
| 10-11 AM | |
| 11-12 AM | |
| 12-1 PM | |
| 1-2 PM | |
| 2-3 PM | |
| 3-4 PM | |
| 4-5 PM | |
| 6-7 PM | |
| 7-8 PM | |
| 8-9 PM | |

## TOP PRIORITIES

## TO DO LIST..

## FOR TOMORROW..

## NOTE..

DATE

QUOTE FOR THE DAY

## TODAY'S SCHEDULE

| 6-7 AM |
| 7-8 AM |
| 8-9 AM |
| 9-10 AM |
| 10-11 AM |
| 11-12 AM |
| 12-1 PM |
| 1-2 PM |
| 2-3 PM |
| 3-4 PM |
| 4-5 PM |
| 6-7 PM |
| 7-8 PM |
| 8-9 PM |

## TOP PRIORITIES

### TO DO LIST..

## FOR TOMORROW..

## NOTE..

DATE

QUOTE FOR THE DAY

## TODAY'S SCHEDULE

| | |
|---|---|
| 6-7 AM | |
| 7-8 AM | |
| 8-9 AM | |
| 9-10 AM | |
| 10-11 AM | |
| 11-12 AM | |
| 12-1 PM | |
| 1-2 PM | |
| 2-3 PM | |
| 3-4 PM | |
| 4-5 PM | |
| 6-7 PM | |
| 7-8 PM | |
| 8-9 PM | |

## TOP PRIORITIES

## TO DO LIST..

## FOR TOMORROW..

## NOTE..

## ODAY'S SCHEDULE

## TOP PRIORITIES

| | |
|---|---|
| 6-7 AM | |
| 7-8 AM | |
| 8-9 AM | |
| 9-10 AM | |
| 10-11 AM | |
| 11-12 AM | |
| 12-1 PM | |
| 1-2 PM | |
| 2-3 PM | |
| 3-4 PM | |
| 4-5 PM | |
| 6-7 PM | |
| 7-8 PM | |
| 8-9 PM | |

## TO DO LIST..

## FOR TOMORROW..

## NOTE..

## TODAY'S SCHEDULE

| | |
|---|---|
| 6-7 AM | |
| 7-8 AM | |
| 8-9 AM | |
| 9-10 AM | |
| 10-11 AM | |
| 11-12 AM | |
| 12-1 PM | |
| 1-2 PM | |
| 2-3 PM | |
| 3-4 PM | |
| 4-5 PM | |
| 6-7 PM | |
| 7-8 PM | |
| 8-9 PM | |

## TOP PRIORITIES

## TO DO LIST..

## FOR TOMORROW..

## NOTE..

QUOTE FOR THE DAY

## TODAY'S SCHEDULE

| 6-7 AM | |
| 7-8 AM | |
| 8-9 AM | |
| 9-10 AM | |
| 10-11 AM | |
| 11-12 AM | |
| 12-1 PM | |
| 1-2 PM | |
| 2-3 PM | |
| 3-4 PM | |
| 4-5 PM | |
| 6-7 PM | |
| 7-8 PM | |
| 8-9 PM | |

## TOP PRIORITIES

### TO DO LIST..

## FOR TOMORROW..

## NOTE..

DATE

QUOTE FOR THE DAY

## TODAY'S SCHEDULE

| | |
|---|---|
| 6-7 AM | |
| 7-8 AM | |
| 8-9 AM | |
| 9-10 AM | |
| 10-11 AM | |
| 11-12 AM | |
| 12-1 PM | |
| 1-2 PM | |
| 2-3 PM | |
| 3-4 PM | |
| 4-5 PM | |
| 6-7 PM | |
| 7-8 PM | |
| 8-9 PM | |

## TOP PRIORITIES

## TO DO LIST..

## FOR TOMORROW..

## NOTE..

## TODAY'S SCHEDULE

## TOP PRIORITIES

| Time | |
|------|--|
| 6-7 AM | |
| 7-8 AM | |
| 8-9 AM | |
| 9-10 AM | |
| 10-11 AM | |
| 11-12 AM | |
| 12-1 PM | |
| 1-2 PM | |
| 2-3 PM | |
| 3-4 PM | |
| 4-5 PM | |
| 6-7 PM | |
| 7-8 PM | |
| 8-9 PM | |

## TO DO LIST..

## FOR TOMORROW..

## NOTE..

## DATE



## TODAY'S SCHEDULE

| | |
|---|---|
| 6-7 AM | |
| 7-8 AM | |
| 8-9 AM | |
| 9-10 AM | |
| 10-11 AM | |
| 11-12 AM | |
| 12-1 PM | |
| 1-2 PM | |
| 2-3 PM | |
| 3-4 PM | |
| 4-5 PM | |
| 6-7 PM | |
| 7-8 PM | |
| 8-9 PM | |

## TOP PRIORITIES

## TO DO LIST..

## FOR TOMORROW..

## NOTE..

## ODAY'S SCHEDULE

6-7 AM

7-8 AM

8-9 AM

9-10 AM

10-11 AM

11-12 AM

12-1 PM

1-2 PM

2-3 PM

3-4 PM

4-5 PM

6-7 PM

7-8 PM

8-9 PM

## TOP PRIORITIES

### TO DO LIST..

## FOR TOMORROW..

## NOTE..

## TODAY'S SCHEDULE

| 6-7 AM | |
| 7-8 AM | |
| 8-9 AM | |
| 9-10 AM | |
| 10-11 AM | |
| 11-12 AM | |
| 12-1 PM | |
| 1-2 PM | |
| 2-3 PM | |
| 3-4 PM | |
| 4-5 PM | |
| 6-7 PM | |
| 7-8 PM | |
| 8-9 PM | |

## TOP PRIORITIES

## TO DO LIST..

## FOR TOMORROW..

## NOTE..

DATE

QUOTE FOR THE DAY

## ODAY'S SCHEDULE

| 6-7 AM | |
| 7-8 AM | |
| 8-9 AM | |
| 9-10 AM | |
| 10-11 AM | |
| 11-12 AM | |
| 12-1 PM | |
| 1-2 PM | |
| 2-3 PM | |
| 3-4 PM | |
| 4-5 PM | |
| 6-7 PM | |
| 7-8 PM | |
| 8-9 PM | |

## TOP PRIORITIES

### TO DO LIST..

## FOR TOMORROW..

## NOTE..

## TODAY'S SCHEDULE

| | |
|---|---|
| 6-7 AM | |
| 7-8 AM | |
| 8-9 AM | |
| 9-10 AM | |
| 10-11 AM | |
| 11-12 AM | |
| 12-1 PM | |
| 1-2 PM | |
| 2-3 PM | |
| 3-4 PM | |
| 4-5 PM | |
| 6-7 PM | |
| 7-8 PM | |
| 8-9 PM | |

## TOP PRIORITIES

## TO DO LIST..

## FOR TOMORROW..

## NOTE..

DATE

QUOTE FOR THE DAY

## TODAY'S SCHEDULE

| 6-7 AM |
| 7-8 AM |
| 8-9 AM |
| 9-10 AM |
| 10-11 AM |
| 11-12 AM |
| 12-1 PM |
| 1-2 PM |
| 2-3 PM |
| 3-4 PM |
| 4-5 PM |
| 6-7 PM |
| 7-8 PM |
| 8-9 PM |

## TOP PRIORITIES

## TO DO LIST..

## FOR TOMORROW..

## NOTE..

DATE

QUOTE FOR THE DAY

## TODAY'S SCHEDULE

| | |
|---|---|
| 6-7 AM | |
| 7-8 AM | |
| 8-9 AM | |
| 9-10 AM | |
| 10-11 AM | |
| 11-12 AM | |
| 12-1 PM | |
| 1-2 PM | |
| 2-3 PM | |
| 3-4 PM | |
| 4-5 PM | |
| 6-7 PM | |
| 7-8 PM | |
| 8-9 PM | |

## TOP PRIORITIES

## TO DO LIST..

## FOR TOMORROW..

## NOTE..

DATE

QUOTE FOR THE DAY

## ODAY'S SCHEDULE

| Time | |
|------|--|
| 6-7 AM | |
| 7-8 AM | |
| 8-9 AM | |
| 9-10 AM | |
| 10-11 AM | |
| 11-12 AM | |
| 12-1 PM | |
| 1-2 PM | |
| 2-3 PM | |
| 3-4 PM | |
| 4-5 PM | |
| 6-7 PM | |
| 7-8 PM | |
| 8-9 PM | |

## TOP PRIORITIES

### TO DO LIST..

☐
☐
☐
☐
☐
☐
☐
☐

## FOR TOMORROW..

## NOTE..

DATE

QUOTE FOR THE DAY

## TODAY'S SCHEDULE

| | |
|---|---|
| 6-7 AM | |
| 7-8 AM | |
| 8-9 AM | |
| 9-10 AM | |
| 10-11 AM | |
| 11-12 AM | |
| 12-1 PM | |
| 1-2 PM | |
| 2-3 PM | |
| 3-4 PM | |
| 4-5 PM | |
| 6-7 PM | |
| 7-8 PM | |
| 8-9 PM | |

## TOP PRIORITIES

## TO DO LIST..

- [ ]
- [ ]
- [ ]
- [ ]
- [ ]
- [ ]
- [ ]
- [ ]

## FOR TOMORROW..

## NOTE..

DATE

QUOTE FOR THE DAY

## TODAY'S SCHEDULE

| 6-7 AM | |
| 7-8 AM | |
| 8-9 AM | |
| 9-10 AM | |
| 10-11 AM | |
| 11-12 AM | |
| 12-1 PM | |
| 1-2 PM | |
| 2-3 PM | |
| 3-4 PM | |
| 4-5 PM | |
| 6-7 PM | |
| 7-8 PM | |
| 8-9 PM | |

## TOP PRIORITIES

## TO DO LIST..

## FOR TOMORROW..

## NOTE..

## TODAY'S SCHEDULE

| | |
|---|---|
| 6-7 AM | |
| 7-8 AM | |
| 8-9 AM | |
| 9-10 AM | |
| 10-11 AM | |
| 11-12 AM | |
| 12-1 PM | |
| 1-2 PM | |
| 2-3 PM | |
| 3-4 PM | |
| 4-5 PM | |
| 6-7 PM | |
| 7-8 PM | |
| 8-9 PM | |

## TOP PRIORITIES

## TO DO LIST..

## FOR TOMORROW..

## NOTE..

# Notes

# Reflection:

# Monthly Planner

Goals

Month:

Notes

| Mon | Tue | Wed | Thu | Fri | Sat | Sun |
|-----|-----|-----|-----|-----|-----|-----|
|  |  |  |  |  |  |  |
|  |  |  |  |  |  |  |
|  |  |  |  |  |  |  |
|  |  |  |  |  |  |  |
|  |  |  |  |  |  |  |

# Book Lists To Read

| ☑ BOOK TITLE | AUTHOR | PROGRESS |
|---|---|---|
| ☐ | | |
| ☐ | | |
| ☐ | | |
| ☐ | | |
| ☐ | | |
| ☐ | | |
| ☐ | | |
| ☐ | | |
| ☐ | | |
| ☐ | | |

## ODAY'S SCHEDULE

6-7 AM

7-8 AM

8-9 AM

9-10 AM

10-11 AM

11-12 AM

12-1 PM

1-2 PM

2-3 PM

3-4 PM

4-5 PM

6-7 PM

7-8 PM

8-9 PM

## TOP PRIORITIES

### TO DO LIST..

## FOR TOMORROW..

## NOTE..

## TODAY'S SCHEDULE

| | |
|---|---|
| 6-7 AM | |
| 7-8 AM | |
| 8-9 AM | |
| 9-10 AM | |
| 10-11 AM | |
| 11-12 AM | |
| 12-1 PM | |
| 1-2 PM | |
| 2-3 PM | |
| 3-4 PM | |
| 4-5 PM | |
| 6-7 PM | |
| 7-8 PM | |
| 8-9 PM | |

## TOP PRIORITIES

## TO DO LIST..

## FOR TOMORROW..

## NOTE..

DATE

QUOTE FOR THE DAY

## ODAY'S SCHEDULE

| 6-7 AM | |
| 7-8 AM | |
| 8-9 AM | |
| 9-10 AM | |
| 10-11 AM | |
| 11-12 AM | |
| 12-1 PM | |
| 1-2 PM | |
| 2-3 PM | |
| 3-4 PM | |
| 4-5 PM | |
| 6-7 PM | |
| 7-8 PM | |
| 8-9 PM | |

## TOP PRIORITIES

### TO DO LIST..

## FOR TOMORROW..

## NOTE..

DATE

QUOTE FOR THE DAY

## TODAY'S SCHEDULE

| | |
|---|---|
| 6-7 AM | |
| 7-8 AM | |
| 8-9 AM | |
| 9-10 AM | |
| 10-11 AM | |
| 11-12 AM | |
| 12-1 PM | |
| 1-2 PM | |
| 2-3 PM | |
| 3-4 PM | |
| 4-5 PM | |
| 6-7 PM | |
| 7-8 PM | |
| 8-9 PM | |

## TOP PRIORITIES

## TO DO LIST..

## FOR TOMORROW..

## NOTE..

DATE

QUOTE FOR THE DAY

## ODAY'S SCHEDULE

| | |
|---|---|
| 6-7 AM | |
| 7-8 AM | |
| 8-9 AM | |
| 9-10 AM | |
| 10-11 AM | |
| 11-12 AM | |
| 12-1 PM | |
| 1-2 PM | |
| 2-3 PM | |
| 3-4 PM | |
| 4-5 PM | |
| 6-7 PM | |
| 7-8 PM | |
| 8-9 PM | |

## TOP PRIORITIES

**TO DO LIST..**

## FOR TOMORROW..

## NOTE..

DATE

QUOTE FOR THE DAY

## TODAY'S SCHEDULE

| 6-7 AM | |
| 7-8 AM | |
| 8-9 AM | |
| 9-10 AM | |
| 10-11 AM | |
| 11-12 AM | |
| 12-1 PM | |
| 1-2 PM | |
| 2-3 PM | |
| 3-4 PM | |
| 4-5 PM | |
| 6-7 PM | |
| 7-8 PM | |
| 8-9 PM | |

## TOP PRIORITIES

## TO DO LIST..

## FOR TOMORROW..

## NOTE..

DATE

QUOTE FOR THE DAY

## TODAY'S SCHEDULE

| | |
|---|---|
| 6-7 AM | |
| 7-8 AM | |
| 8-9 AM | |
| 9-10 AM | |
| 10-11 AM | |
| 11-12 AM | |
| 12-1 PM | |
| 1-2 PM | |
| 2-3 PM | |
| 3-4 PM | |
| 4-5 PM | |
| 6-7 PM | |
| 7-8 PM | |
| 8-9 PM | |

## TOP PRIORITIES

### TO DO LIST..

☐
☐
☐
☐
☐
☐
☐
☐

## FOR TOMORROW..

## NOTE..

DATE

QUOTE FOR THE DAY

## TODAY'S SCHEDULE

| 6-7 AM | |
| 7-8 AM | |
| 8-9 AM | |
| 9-10 AM | |
| 10-11 AM | |
| 11-12 AM | |
| 12-1 PM | |
| 1-2 PM | |
| 2-3 PM | |
| 3-4 PM | |
| 4-5 PM | |
| 6-7 PM | |
| 7-8 PM | |
| 8-9 PM | |

## TOP PRIORITIES

## TO DO LIST..

## FOR TOMORROW..

## NOTE..

DATE

QUOTE FOR THE DAY

## ODAY'S SCHEDULE

TOP PRIORITIES

6-7 AM

7-8 AM

8-9 AM

9-10 AM

10-11 AM

11-12 AM

12-1 PM

1-2 PM

2-3 PM

3-4 PM

4-5 PM

6-7 PM

7-8 PM

8-9 PM

### TO DO LIST..

## FOR TOMORROW..

## NOTE..

DATE

QUOTE FOR THE DAY

## TODAY'S SCHEDULE

| | |
|---|---|
| 6-7 AM | |
| 7-8 AM | |
| 8-9 AM | |
| 9-10 AM | |
| 10-11 AM | |
| 11-12 AM | |
| 12-1 PM | |
| 1-2 PM | |
| 2-3 PM | |
| 3-4 PM | |
| 4-5 PM | |
| 6-7 PM | |
| 7-8 PM | |
| 8-9 PM | |

## TOP PRIORITIES

## TO DO LIST..

## FOR TOMORROW..

## NOTE..

DATE

QUOTE FOR THE DAY

## ODAY'S SCHEDULE

| 6-7 AM |
| 7-8 AM |
| 8-9 AM |
| 9-10 AM |
| 10-11 AM |
| 11-12 AM |
| 12-1 PM |
| 1-2 PM |
| 2-3 PM |
| 3-4 PM |
| 4-5 PM |
| 6-7 PM |
| 7-8 PM |
| 8-9 PM |

## TOP PRIORITIES

## TO DO LIST..

## FOR TOMORROW..

## NOTE..

DATE

QUOTE FOR THE DAY

## TODAY'S SCHEDULE

| 6-7 AM | |
| 7-8 AM | |
| 8-9 AM | |
| 9-10 AM | |
| 10-11 AM | |
| 11-12 AM | |
| 12-1 PM | |
| 1-2 PM | |
| 2-3 PM | |
| 3-4 PM | |
| 4-5 PM | |
| 6-7 PM | |
| 7-8 PM | |
| 8-9 PM | |

## TOP PRIORITIES

## TO DO LIST..

☐
☐
☐
☐
☐
☐
☐
☐

## FOR TOMORROW..

## NOTE..

DATE

QUOTE FOR THE DAY

## TODAY'S SCHEDULE

| | |
|---|---|
| 6-7 AM | |
| 7-8 AM | |
| 8-9 AM | |
| 9-10 AM | |
| 10-11 AM | |
| 11-12 AM | |
| 12-1 PM | |
| 1-2 PM | |
| 2-3 PM | |
| 3-4 PM | |
| 4-5 PM | |
| 6-7 PM | |
| 7-8 PM | |
| 8-9 PM | |

## TOP PRIORITIES

## TO DO LIST..

## FOR TOMORROW..

## NOTE..

DATE

QUOTE FOR THE DAY

## TODAY'S SCHEDULE

| | |
|---|---|
| 6-7 AM | |
| 7-8 AM | |
| 8-9 AM | |
| 9-10 AM | |
| 10-11 AM | |
| 11-12 AM | |
| 12-1 PM | |
| 1-2 PM | |
| 2-3 PM | |
| 3-4 PM | |
| 4-5 PM | |
| 6-7 PM | |
| 7-8 PM | |
| 8-9 PM | |

## TOP PRIORITIES

## TO DO LIST..

## FOR TOMORROW..

## NOTE..

DATE

QUOTE FOR THE DAY

## ODAY'S SCHEDULE

| | |
|---|---|
| 6-7 AM | |
| 7-8 AM | |
| 8-9 AM | |
| 9-10 AM | |
| 10-11 AM | |
| 11-12 AM | |
| 12-1 PM | |
| 1-2 PM | |
| 2-3 PM | |
| 3-4 PM | |
| 4-5 PM | |
| 6-7 PM | |
| 7-8 PM | |
| 8-9 PM | |

## TOP PRIORITIES

### TO DO LIST..

## FOR TOMORROW..

## NOTE..

DATE

QUOTE FOR THE DAY

## TODAY'S SCHEDULE

| | |
|---|---|
| 6-7 AM | |
| 7-8 AM | |
| 8-9 AM | |
| 9-10 AM | |
| 10-11 AM | |
| 11-12 AM | |
| 12-1 PM | |
| 1-2 PM | |
| 2-3 PM | |
| 3-4 PM | |
| 4-5 PM | |
| 6-7 PM | |
| 7-8 PM | |
| 8-9 PM | |

## TOP PRIORITIES

FOR TOMORROW..

## ODAY'S SCHEDULE

| | |
|---|---|
| 6-7 AM | |
| 7-8 AM | |
| 8-9 AM | |
| 9-10 AM | |
| 10-11 AM | |
| 11-12 AM | |
| 12-1 PM | |
| 1-2 PM | |
| 2-3 PM | |
| 3-4 PM | |
| 4-5 PM | |
| 6-7 PM | |
| 7-8 PM | |
| 8-9 PM | |

## TOP PRIORITIES

## TO DO LIST..

## FOR TOMORROW..

## NOTE..

DATE

QUOTE FOR THE DAY

## TODAY'S SCHEDULE

| 6-7 AM | |
| 7-8 AM | |
| 8-9 AM | |
| 9-10 AM | |
| 10-11 AM | |
| 11-12 AM | |
| 12-1 PM | |
| 1-2 PM | |
| 2-3 PM | |
| 3-4 PM | |
| 4-5 PM | |
| 6-7 PM | |
| 7-8 PM | |
| 8-9 PM | |

## TOP PRIORITIES

### TO DO LIST..

### FOR TOMORROW..

### NOTE..

DATE

QUOTE FOR THE DAY

## TODAY'S SCHEDULE

| | |
|---|---|
| 6-7 AM | |
| 7-8 AM | |
| 8-9 AM | |
| 9-10 AM | |
| 10-11 AM | |
| 11-12 AM | |
| 12-1 PM | |
| 1-2 PM | |
| 2-3 PM | |
| 3-4 PM | |
| 4-5 PM | |
| 6-7 PM | |
| 7-8 PM | |
| 8-9 PM | |

## TOP PRIORITIES

### TO DO LIST..

## FOR TOMORROW..

## NOTE..

DATE

QUOTE FOR THE DAY

## TODAY'S SCHEDULE

| | |
|---|---|
| 6-7 AM | |
| 7-8 AM | |
| 8-9 AM | |
| 9-10 AM | |
| 10-11 AM | |
| 11-12 AM | |
| 12-1 PM | |
| 1-2 PM | |
| 2-3 PM | |
| 3-4 PM | |
| 4-5 PM | |
| 6-7 PM | |
| 7-8 PM | |
| 8-9 PM | |

## TOP PRIORITIES

## TO DO LIST..

## FOR TOMORROW..

## NOTE..

QUOTE FOR THE DAY

## TODAY'S SCHEDULE

| | |
|---|---|
| 6-7 AM | |
| 7-8 AM | |
| 8-9 AM | |
| 9-10 AM | |
| 10-11 AM | |
| 11-12 AM | |
| 12-1 PM | |
| 1-2 PM | |
| 2-3 PM | |
| 3-4 PM | |
| 4-5 PM | |
| 6-7 PM | |
| 7-8 PM | |
| 8-9 PM | |

## TOP PRIORITIES

## TO DO LIST..

## FOR TOMORROW..

## NOTE..

DATE

QUOTE FOR THE DAY

## TODAY'S SCHEDULE

| | |
|---|---|
| 6-7 AM | |
| 7-8 AM | |
| 8-9 AM | |
| 9-10 AM | |
| 10-11 AM | |
| 11-12 AM | |
| 12-1 PM | |
| 1-2 PM | |
| 2-3 PM | |
| 3-4 PM | |
| 4-5 PM | |
| 6-7 PM | |
| 7-8 PM | |
| 8-9 PM | |

## TOP PRIORITIES

## FOR TOMORROW..

## NOTE..

DATE

QUOTE FOR THE DAY

## TODAY'S SCHEDULE

| | |
|---|---|
| 6-7 AM | |
| 7-8 AM | |
| 8-9 AM | |
| 9-10 AM | |
| 10-11 AM | |
| 11-12 AM | |
| 12-1 PM | |
| 1-2 PM | |
| 2-3 PM | |
| 3-4 PM | |
| 4-5 PM | |
| 6-7 PM | |
| 7-8 PM | |
| 8-9 PM | |

## TOP PRIORITIES

### TO DO LIST..

☐
☐
☐
☐
☐
☐
☐
☐

## FOR TOMORROW..

## NOTE..

DATE

QUOTE FOR THE DAY

## TODAY'S SCHEDULE

| | |
|---|---|
| 6-7 AM | |
| 7-8 AM | |
| 8-9 AM | |
| 9-10 AM | |
| 10-11 AM | |
| 11-12 AM | |
| 12-1 PM | |
| 1-2 PM | |
| 2-3 PM | |
| 3-4 PM | |
| 4-5 PM | |
| 6-7 PM | |
| 7-8 PM | |
| 8-9 PM | |

## TOP PRIORITIES

TO DO LIST..

FOR TOMORROW..

NOTE..

DATE

QUOTE FOR THE DAY

## TODAY'S SCHEDULE

| | |
|---|---|
| 6-7 AM | |
| 7-8 AM | |
| 8-9 AM | |
| 9-10 AM | |
| 10-11 AM | |
| 11-12 AM | |
| 12-1 PM | |
| 1-2 PM | |
| 2-3 PM | |
| 3-4 PM | |
| 4-5 PM | |
| 6-7 PM | |
| 7-8 PM | |
| 8-9 PM | |

## TOP PRIORITIES

### TO DO LIST..

☐
☐
☐
☐
☐
☐
☐
☐

## FOR TOMORROW..

## NOTE..

DATE

QUOTE FOR THE DAY

## TODAY'S SCHEDULE

| | |
|---|---|
| 6-7 AM | |
| 7-8 AM | |
| 8-9 AM | |
| 9-10 AM | |
| 10-11 AM | |
| 11-12 AM | |
| 12-1 PM | |
| 1-2 PM | |
| 2-3 PM | |
| 3-4 PM | |
| 4-5 PM | |
| 6-7 PM | |
| 7-8 PM | |
| 8-9 PM | |

## TOP PRIORITIES

### TO DO LIST..

- ☐
- ☐
- ☐
- ☐
- ☐
- ☐
- ☐
- ☐

## FOR TOMORROW..

## NOTE..

QUOTE FOR THE DAY

## ODAY'S SCHEDULE

| | |
|---|---|
| 6-7 AM | |
| 7-8 AM | |
| 8-9 AM | |
| 9-10 AM | |
| 10-11 AM | |
| 11-12 AM | |
| 12-1 PM | |
| 1-2 PM | |
| 2-3 PM | |
| 3-4 PM | |
| 4-5 PM | |
| 6-7 PM | |
| 7-8 PM | |
| 8-9 PM | |

## TOP PRIORITIES

### TO DO LIST..

## FOR TOMORROW..

## NOTE..

DATE

QUOTE FOR THE DAY

## TODAY'S SCHEDULE

| 6-7 AM | |
| 7-8 AM | |
| 8-9 AM | |
| 9-10 AM | |
| 10-11 AM | |
| 11-12 AM | |
| 12-1 PM | |
| 1-2 PM | |
| 2-3 PM | |
| 3-4 PM | |
| 4-5 PM | |
| 6-7 PM | |
| 7-8 PM | |
| 8-9 PM | |

## TOP PRIORITIES

## TO DO LIST..

## FOR TOMORROW..

## NOTE..

## ODAY'S SCHEDULE

| | |
|---|---|
| 6-7 AM | |
| 7-8 AM | |
| 8-9 AM | |
| 9-10 AM | |
| 10-11 AM | |
| 11-12 AM | |
| 12-1 PM | |
| 1-2 PM | |
| 2-3 PM | |
| 3-4 PM | |
| 4-5 PM | |
| 6-7 PM | |
| 7-8 PM | |
| 8-9 PM | |

## TOP PRIORITIES

### TO DO LIST..

## FOR TOMORROW..

## NOTE..

## TODAY'S SCHEDULE

| | |
|---|---|
| 6-7 AM | |
| 7-8 AM | |
| 8-9 AM | |
| 9-10 AM | |
| 10-11 AM | |
| 11-12 AM | |
| 12-1 PM | |
| 1-2 PM | |
| 2-3 PM | |
| 3-4 PM | |
| 4-5 PM | |
| 6-7 PM | |
| 7-8 PM | |
| 8-9 PM | |

## TOP PRIORITIES

## TO DO LIST..

## FOR TOMORROW..

## NOTE..

DATE

QUOTE FOR THE DAY

## TODAY'S SCHEDULE

TOP PRIORITIES

| | |
|---|---|
| 6-7 AM | |
| 7-8 AM | |
| 8-9 AM | |
| 9-10 AM | |
| 10-11 AM | |
| 11-12 AM | |
| 12-1 PM | |
| 1-2 PM | |
| 2-3 PM | |
| 3-4 PM | |
| 4-5 PM | |
| 6-7 PM | |
| 7-8 PM | |
| 8-9 PM | |

## TO DO LIST..

☐
☐
☐
☐
☐
☐
☐
☐

## FOR TOMORROW..

## NOTE..

# Notes

# Reflection:

# Monthly Planner

Goals

Month:

Notes

| Mon | Tue | Wed | Thu | Fri | Sat | Sun |
|-----|-----|-----|-----|-----|-----|-----|
|  |  |  |  |  |  |  |
|  |  |  |  |  |  |  |
|  |  |  |  |  |  |  |
|  |  |  |  |  |  |  |
|  |  |  |  |  |  |  |

# Book Lists To Read

| ✓ | BOOK TITLE | AUTHOR | PROGRESS |
|---|---|---|---|
| | | | |
| | | | |
| | | | |
| | | | |
| | | | |
| | | | |
| | | | |
| | | | |
| | | | |
| | | | |
| | | | |

## TODAY'S SCHEDULE

| | |
|---|---|
| 6-7 AM | |
| 7-8 AM | |
| 8-9 AM | |
| 9-10 AM | |
| 10-11 AM | |
| 11-12 AM | |
| 12-1 PM | |
| 1-2 PM | |
| 2-3 PM | |
| 3-4 PM | |
| 4-5 PM | |
| 6-7 PM | |
| 7-8 PM | |
| 8-9 PM | |

## TOP PRIORITIES

## TO DO LIST..

## FOR TOMORROW..

## NOTE..

## TODAY'S SCHEDULE

TOP PRIORITIES

| 6-7 AM | |
| 7-8 AM | |
| 8-9 AM | |
| 9-10 AM | |
| 10-11 AM | |
| 11-12 AM | |
| 12-1 PM | |
| 1-2 PM | |
| 2-3 PM | |
| 3-4 PM | |
| 4-5 PM | |
| 6-7 PM | |
| 7-8 PM | |
| 8-9 PM | |

## TO DO LIST..

## FOR TOMORROW..

## NOTE..

## TODAY'S SCHEDULE

| | |
|---|---|
| 6-7 AM | |
| 7-8 AM | |
| 8-9 AM | |
| 9-10 AM | |
| 10-11 AM | |
| 11-12 AM | |
| 12-1 PM | |
| 1-2 PM | |
| 2-3 PM | |
| 3-4 PM | |
| 4-5 PM | |
| 6-7 PM | |
| 7-8 PM | |
| 8-9 PM | |

## TOP PRIORITIES

## TO DO LIST..

## FOR TOMORROW..

## NOTE..

DATE

QUOTE FOR THE DAY

## ODAY'S SCHEDULE

| 6-7 AM |
| 7-8 AM |
| 8-9 AM |
| 9-10 AM |
| 10-11 AM |
| 11-12 AM |
| 12-1 PM |
| 1-2 PM |
| 2-3 PM |
| 3-4 PM |
| 4-5 PM |
| 6-7 PM |
| 7-8 PM |
| 8-9 PM |

## TOP PRIORITIES

TO DO LIST..

## FOR TOMORROW..

## NOTE..

DATE

QUOTE FOR THE DAY

## TODAY'S SCHEDULE

|  | |
|---|---|
| 6-7 AM | |
| 7-8 AM | |
| 8-9 AM | |
| 9-10 AM | |
| 10-11 AM | |
| 11-12 AM | |
| 12-1 PM | |
| 1-2 PM | |
| 2-3 PM | |
| 3-4 PM | |
| 4-5 PM | |
| 6-7 PM | |
| 7-8 PM | |
| 8-9 PM | |

## TOP PRIORITIES

TO DO LIST..

FOR TOMORROW..

NOTE..

DATE

QUOTE FOR THE DAY

## TODAY'S SCHEDULE

| | |
|---|---|
| 6-7 AM | |
| 7-8 AM | |
| 8-9 AM | |
| 9-10 AM | |
| 10-11 AM | |
| 11-12 AM | |
| 12-1 PM | |
| 1-2 PM | |
| 2-3 PM | |
| 3-4 PM | |
| 4-5 PM | |
| 6-7 PM | |
| 7-8 PM | |
| 8-9 PM | |

## TOP PRIORITIES

## TO DO LIST..

☐
☐
☐
☐
☐
☐
☐
☐

## FOR TOMORROW..

## NOTE..

DATE

QUOTE FOR THE DAY

## TODAY'S SCHEDULE

| | |
|---|---|
| 6-7 AM | |
| 7-8 AM | |
| 8-9 AM | |
| 9-10 AM | |
| 10-11 AM | |
| 11-12 AM | |
| 12-1 PM | |
| 1-2 PM | |
| 2-3 PM | |
| 3-4 PM | |
| 4-5 PM | |
| 6-7 PM | |
| 7-8 PM | |
| 8-9 PM | |

## TOP PRIORITIES

FOR TOMORROW..

NOTE..

DATE

QUOTE FOR THE DAY

## TODAY'S SCHEDULE

| | |
|---|---|
| 6-7 AM | |
| 7-8 AM | |
| 8-9 AM | |
| 9-10 AM | |
| 10-11 AM | |
| 11-12 AM | |
| 12-1 PM | |
| 1-2 PM | |
| 2-3 PM | |
| 3-4 PM | |
| 4-5 PM | |
| 6-7 PM | |
| 7-8 PM | |
| 8-9 PM | |

## TOP PRIORITIES

### TO DO LIST..

☐
☐
☐
☐
☐
☐
☐
☐

## FOR TOMORROW..

## NOTE..

QUOTE FOR THE DAY

## TODAY'S SCHEDULE

| 6-7 AM | |
| 7-8 AM | |
| 8-9 AM | |
| 9-10 AM | |
| 10-11 AM | |
| 11-12 AM | |
| 12-1 PM | |
| 1-2 PM | |
| 2-3 PM | |
| 3-4 PM | |
| 4-5 PM | |
| 6-7 PM | |
| 7-8 PM | |
| 8-9 PM | |

## TOP PRIORITIES

## TO DO LIST..

☐
☐
☐
☐
☐
☐
☐
☐

## FOR TOMORROW..

## NOTE..

DATE

QUOTE FOR THE DAY

## ODAY'S SCHEDULE

TOP PRIORITIES

6-7 AM

7-8 AM

8-9 AM

9-10 AM

10-11 AM

11-12 AM

12-1 PM

1-2 PM

2-3 PM

3-4 PM

4-5 PM

6-7 PM

7-8 PM

8-9 PM

## TO DO LIST..

## FOR TOMORROW..

## NOTE..

DATE

QUOTE FOR THE DAY

## TODAY'S SCHEDULE

| | |
|---|---|
| 6-7 AM | |
| 7-8 AM | |
| 8-9 AM | |
| 9-10 AM | |
| 10-11 AM | |
| 11-12 AM | |
| 12-1 PM | |
| 1-2 PM | |
| 2-3 PM | |
| 3-4 PM | |
| 4-5 PM | |
| 6-7 PM | |
| 7-8 PM | |
| 8-9 PM | |

## TOP PRIORITIES

## FOR TOMORROW..

NOTE..

DATE

QUOTE FOR THE DAY

## TODAY'S SCHEDULE

|  | |
|---|---|
| 6-7 AM | |
| 7-8 AM | |
| 8-9 AM | |
| 9-10 AM | |
| 10-11 AM | |
| 11-12 AM | |
| 12-1 PM | |
| 1-2 PM | |
| 2-3 PM | |
| 3-4 PM | |
| 4-5 PM | |
| 6-7 PM | |
| 7-8 PM | |
| 8-9 PM | |

## TOP PRIORITIES

### TO DO LIST..

☐
☐
☐
☐
☐
☐
☐
☐

## FOR TOMORROW..

## NOTE..

## TODAY'S SCHEDULE

| 6-7 AM | |
| 7-8 AM | |
| 8-9 AM | |
| 9-10 AM | |
| 10-11 AM | |
| 11-12 AM | |
| 12-1 PM | |
| 1-2 PM | |
| 2-3 PM | |
| 3-4 PM | |
| 4-5 PM | |
| 6-7 PM | |
| 7-8 PM | |
| 8-9 PM | |

## TOP PRIORITIES

## FOR TOMORROW..

DATE

QUOTE FOR THE DAY

## TODAY'S SCHEDULE

| 6-7 AM |
| 7-8 AM |
| 8-9 AM |
| 9-10 AM |
| 10-11 AM |
| 11-12 AM |
| 12-1 PM |
| 1-2 PM |
| 2-3 PM |
| 3-4 PM |
| 4-5 PM |
| 6-7 PM |
| 7-8 PM |
| 8-9 PM |

## TOP PRIORITIES

### TO DO LIST..

## FOR TOMORROW..

## NOTE..

QUOTE FOR THE DAY

## TODAY'S SCHEDULE

| 6-7 AM | |
| 7-8 AM | |
| 8-9 AM | |
| 9-10 AM | |
| 10-11 AM | |
| 11-12 AM | |
| 12-1 PM | |
| 1-2 PM | |
| 2-3 PM | |
| 3-4 PM | |
| 4-5 PM | |
| 6-7 PM | |
| 7-8 PM | |
| 8-9 PM | |

## TOP PRIORITIES

## TO DO LIST..

## FOR TOMORROW..

## NOTE..

QUOTE FOR THE DAY

## TODAY'S SCHEDULE

6-7 AM

7-8 AM

8-9 AM

9-10 AM

10-11 AM

11-12 AM

12-1 PM

1-2 PM

2-3 PM

3-4 PM

4-5 PM

6-7 PM

7-8 PM

8-9 PM

## TOP PRIORITIES

### TO DO LIST..

## FOR TOMORROW..

## NOTE..

DATE

QUOTE FOR THE DAY

## TODAY'S SCHEDULE

| 6-7 AM | |
| 7-8 AM | |
| 8-9 AM | |
| 9-10 AM | |
| 10-11 AM | |
| 11-12 AM | |
| 12-1 PM | |
| 1-2 PM | |
| 2-3 PM | |
| 3-4 PM | |
| 4-5 PM | |
| 6-7 PM | |
| 7-8 PM | |
| 8-9 PM | |

## TOP PRIORITIES

## FOR TOMORROW..

## NOTE..

DATE

QUOTE FOR THE DAY

## TODAY'S SCHEDULE

| | |
|---|---|
| 6-7 AM | |
| 7-8 AM | |
| 8-9 AM | |
| 9-10 AM | |
| 10-11 AM | |
| 11-12 AM | |
| 12-1 PM | |
| 1-2 PM | |
| 2-3 PM | |
| 3-4 PM | |
| 4-5 PM | |
| 6-7 PM | |
| 7-8 PM | |
| 8-9 PM | |

## TOP PRIORITIES

### TO DO LIST..

## FOR TOMORROW..

## NOTE..

DATE

QUOTE FOR THE DAY

## TODAY'S SCHEDULE

|  | |
|---|---|
| 6-7 AM | |
| 7-8 AM | |
| 8-9 AM | |
| 9-10 AM | |
| 10-11 AM | |
| 11-12 AM | |
| 12-1 PM | |
| 1-2 PM | |
| 2-3 PM | |
| 3-4 PM | |
| 4-5 PM | |
| 6-7 PM | |
| 7-8 PM | |
| 8-9 PM | |

## TOP PRIORITIES

### TO DO LIST..

- ☐
- ☐
- ☐
- ☐
- ☐
- ☐
- ☐
- ☐

## FOR TOMORROW..

## NOTE..

DATE

QUOTE FOR THE DAY

## TODAY'S SCHEDULE

| 6-7 AM |
| 7-8 AM |
| 8-9 AM |
| 9-10 AM |
| 10-11 AM |
| 11-12 AM |
| 12-1 PM |
| 1-2 PM |
| 2-3 PM |
| 3-4 PM |
| 4-5 PM |
| 6-7 PM |
| 7-8 PM |
| 8-9 PM |

## TOP PRIORITIES

## TO DO LIST..

## FOR TOMORROW..

## NOTE..

## TODAY'S SCHEDULE

| 6-7 AM | |
| 7-8 AM | |
| 8-9 AM | |
| 9-10 AM | |
| 10-11 AM | |
| 11-12 AM | |
| 12-1 PM | |
| 1-2 PM | |
| 2-3 PM | |
| 3-4 PM | |
| 4-5 PM | |
| 6-7 PM | |
| 7-8 PM | |
| 8-9 PM | |

## TOP PRIORITIES

### TO DO LIST..

### FOR TOMORROW..

### NOTE..

## ODAY'S SCHEDULE

6-7 AM

7-8 AM

8-9 AM

9-10 AM

10-11 AM

11-12 AM

12-1 PM

1-2 PM

2-3 PM

3-4 PM

4-5 PM

6-7 PM

7-8 PM

8-9 PM

## TOP PRIORITIES

### TO DO LIST..

## FOR TOMORROW..

## NOTE..

## TODAY'S SCHEDULE

| Time | |
|------|--|
| 6-7 AM | |
| 7-8 AM | |
| 8-9 AM | |
| 9-10 AM | |
| 10-11 AM | |
| 11-12 AM | |
| 12-1 PM | |
| 1-2 PM | |
| 2-3 PM | |
| 3-4 PM | |
| 4-5 PM | |
| 6-7 PM | |
| 7-8 PM | |
| 8-9 PM | |

## TOP PRIORITIES

## TO DO LIST..

## FOR TOMORROW..

## NOTE..

DATE

QUOTE FOR THE DAY

## TODAY'S SCHEDULE

| | |
|---|---|
| 6-7 AM | |
| 7-8 AM | |
| 8-9 AM | |
| 9-10 AM | |
| 10-11 AM | |
| 11-12 AM | |
| 12-1 PM | |
| 1-2 PM | |
| 2-3 PM | |
| 3-4 PM | |
| 4-5 PM | |
| 6-7 PM | |
| 7-8 PM | |
| 8-9 PM | |

## TOP PRIORITIES

## TO DO LIST..

## FOR TOMORROW..

## NOTE..

DATE

QUOTE FOR THE DAY

## TODAY'S SCHEDULE

| | |
|---|---|
| 6-7 AM | |
| 7-8 AM | |
| 8-9 AM | |
| 9-10 AM | |
| 10-11 AM | |
| 11-12 AM | |
| 12-1 PM | |
| 1-2 PM | |
| 2-3 PM | |
| 3-4 PM | |
| 4-5 PM | |
| 6-7 PM | |
| 7-8 PM | |
| 8-9 PM | |

## TOP PRIORITIES

## FOR TOMORROW..

DATE

QUOTE FOR THE DAY

## TODAY'S SCHEDULE

| | |
|---|---|
| 6-7 AM | |
| 7-8 AM | |
| 8-9 AM | |
| 9-10 AM | |
| 10-11 AM | |
| 11-12 AM | |
| 12-1 PM | |
| 1-2 PM | |
| 2-3 PM | |
| 3-4 PM | |
| 4-5 PM | |
| 6-7 PM | |
| 7-8 PM | |
| 8-9 PM | |

## TOP PRIORITIES

### TO DO LIST..

## FOR TOMORROW..

## NOTE..

## TODAY'S SCHEDULE

| | |
|---|---|
| 6-7 AM | |
| 7-8 AM | |
| 8-9 AM | |
| 9-10 AM | |
| 10-11 AM | |
| 11-12 AM | |
| 12-1 PM | |
| 1-2 PM | |
| 2-3 PM | |
| 3-4 PM | |
| 4-5 PM | |
| 6-7 PM | |
| 7-8 PM | |
| 8-9 PM | |

## TOP PRIORITIES

## TO DO LIST..

## FOR TOMORROW..

## NOTE..

DATE

QUOTE FOR THE DAY

## ODAY'S SCHEDULE

| | |
|---|---|
| 6-7 AM | |
| 7-8 AM | |
| 8-9 AM | |
| 9-10 AM | |
| 10-11 AM | |
| 11-12 AM | |
| 12-1 PM | |
| 1-2 PM | |
| 2-3 PM | |
| 3-4 PM | |
| 4-5 PM | |
| 6-7 PM | |
| 7-8 PM | |
| 8-9 PM | |

## TOP PRIORITIES

TO DO LIST..

## FOR TOMORROW..

NOTE..

DATE

QUOTE FOR THE DAY

## TODAY'S SCHEDULE

| | |
|---|---|
| 6-7 AM | |
| 7-8 AM | |
| 8-9 AM | |
| 9-10 AM | |
| 10-11 AM | |
| 11-12 AM | |
| 12-1 PM | |
| 1-2 PM | |
| 2-3 PM | |
| 3-4 PM | |
| 4-5 PM | |
| 6-7 PM | |
| 7-8 PM | |
| 8-9 PM | |

## TOP PRIORITIES

## TO DO LIST..

☐
☐
☐
☐
☐
☐
☐
☐

## FOR TOMORROW..

## NOTE..

DATE

QUOTE FOR THE DAY

## TODAY'S SCHEDULE

| | |
|---|---|
| 6-7 AM | |
| 7-8 AM | |
| 8-9 AM | |
| 9-10 AM | |
| 10-11 AM | |
| 11-12 AM | |
| 12-1 PM | |
| 1-2 PM | |
| 2-3 PM | |
| 3-4 PM | |
| 4-5 PM | |
| 6-7 PM | |
| 7-8 PM | |
| 8-9 PM | |

## TOP PRIORITIES

### TO DO LIST..

☐
☐
☐
☐
☐
☐
☐
☐

## FOR TOMORROW..

## NOTE..

QUOTE FOR THE DAY

## TODAY'S SCHEDULE

| | |
|---|---|
| 6-7 AM | |
| 7-8 AM | |
| 8-9 AM | |
| 9-10 AM | |
| 10-11 AM | |
| 11-12 AM | |
| 12-1 PM | |
| 1-2 PM | |
| 2-3 PM | |
| 3-4 PM | |
| 4-5 PM | |
| 6-7 PM | |
| 7-8 PM | |
| 8-9 PM | |

## TOP PRIORITIES

## FOR TOMORROW..

NOTE..

# Notes

# Reflection:

|  |  |  |
|---|---|---|
| JANUARY | FEBRUARY | MARCH |
| APRIL | MAY | JUNE |
| JULY | AUGUST | SEPTEMBER |
| OCTOBER | NOVEMBER | DECEMBER |

# CONTACT LIST

Name:

Phone No.:

Email Address:

Notes:

Name:

Phone No.:

Email Address:

Notes:

Name:

Phone No.:

Email Address:

Notes:

Name:

Phone No.:

Email Address:

Notes:

Name:

Phone No.:

Email Address:

Notes:

Name:

Phone No.:

Email Address:

Notes:

Name:

Phone No.:

Email Address:

Notes:

Name:

Phone No.:

Email Address:

Notes:

Name:

Phone No.:

Email Address:

Notes:

Name:

Phone No.:

Email Address:

Notes:

# CONTACT LIST

Name:

Phone No.:

Email Address:

Notes:

Name:

Phone No.:

Email Address:

Notes:

Name:

Phone No.:

Email Address:

Notes:

Name:

Phone No.:

Email Address:

Notes:

Name:

Phone No.:

Email Address:

Notes:

Name:

Phone No.:

Email Address:

Notes:

Name:

Phone No.:

Email Address:

Notes:

Name:

Phone No.:

Email Address:

Notes:

Name:

Phone No.:

Email Address:

Notes:

Name:

Phone No.:

Email Address:

Notes:

# Notes

# Notes

# Reflection

# Reflection:

www.ingramcontent.com/pod-product-compliance
Lightning Source LLC
Chambersburg PA
CBHW070904250726
48662CB00003B/1502